Madagascar

Madagascar
History of the Great Island

Collection

LM Publishers

Chapter 1

I[1]

Madagascar, the Great Britain of Africa, is a great island situated about 250 miles from the east coast of Africa, and extends from 12° to 25½° S. latitude. It is almost 1,000 miles long, with an extreme width of 360 and an average width of more than 260 miles. A lofty granitic plateau, from eighty to 160 miles wide and from 3,000 to 5,000 feet high, occupies its central portion, on which rise peaks and domes of basalt and granite to a height of nearly 9,000 feet; and there are also numerous extinct volcanic cones and craters.

All round the island, but especially developed on the south and west, are plains of a few hundred feet elevation, formed of rocks which are shown by their fossils to be of Jurassic age, or at all events to belong to somewhere near the middle portion of the Secondary period. The higher granitic plateau

---

[1] Based on the work of Alfred R. Wallace.

consists of bare undulating moors, while the lower Secondary plains are more or less wooded; and there is here also a continuous belt of dense forest, varying from six or eight to fifty miles wide, encircling the whole island, usually at about thirty miles distance from the coast but in the north-east coming down to the sea-shore.

The sea around Madagascar, when the shallow bank on which it stands is passed, is generally deep. This 100-fathom bank is only from one to three miles wide on the east side, but on the west it is much broader, and stretches out opposite Mozambique to a distance of about eighty miles.

The Mozambique Channel is rather more than 1,000 fathoms deep, but there is only a narrow belt of this depth opposite Mozambique, and still narrower where the Comoro Islands and adjacent shoals seem to form stepping-stones to the continent of Africa. The 1,000-fathom line includes Aldabra and the small Farquhar Islands to the north of Madagascar; while to the east the sea deepens rapidly to the 1,000-fathom line and then more slowly, a profound channel of 2,400 fathoms separating Madagascar from Bourbon and Mauritius. To the north-east of Mauritius are a series of extensive shoals forming four large banks less than 100 fathoms below the surface, while the 1,000-fathom line includes them all, with an area about half that of Madagascar itself. A little further north is the Seychelles group, also standing on an extensive 1,000-fathom bank, while all round the sea is more than 2,000 fathoms deep.

It seems probable, then, that to the north-east of Madagascar there was once a series of very large islands, separated from it by not very wide straits; while eastward across the Indian Ocean we find the Chagos and Maldive coral atolls, perhaps marking the position of other large islands, which together would form a line of communication, by comparatively easy stages of 400 or 500 miles each between Madagascar and India. These submerged islands are of great importance in explaining some anomalous features in the zoology of this great island.

If the rocks of Secondary age which form a belt around the island are held to indicate that Madagascar was once of less extent than it is now (though this by no means necessarily follows), we have also evidence that it has recently been considerably larger; for along the east coast there is an extensive barrier coral-reef about 350 miles in length, and varying in distance from the land from a quarter of a mile to three or four miles. This seems to indicate recent subsidence; while we have no record of raised coral rocks inland which would certainly mark any recent elevation, though fringing coral reefs surround a considerable portion of the northern, eastern, and south-western coasts. We may therefore conclude that during Tertiary times the island was usually as large as, and often probably much larger than, it is now.

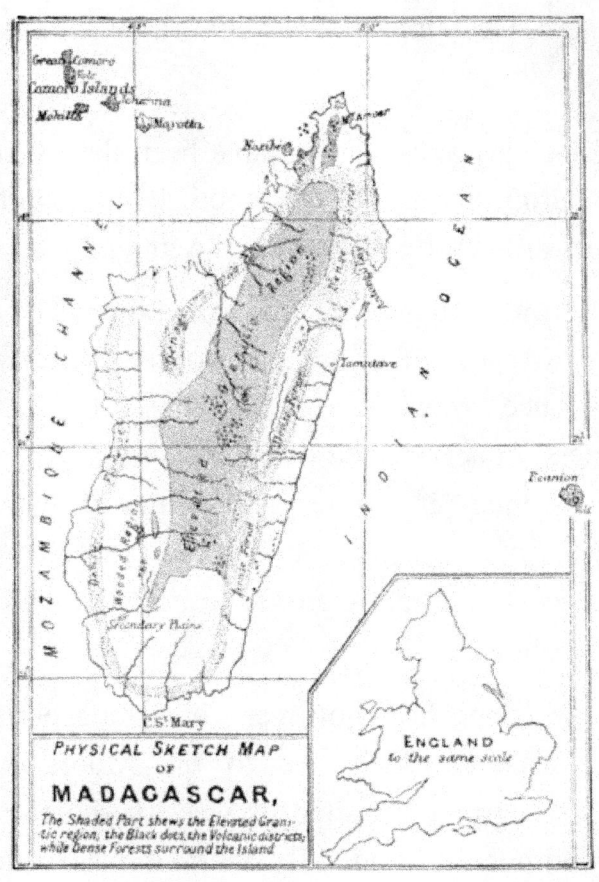

II

The Discovery of Madagascar [2]

Madagascar is said to have been discovered by Europeans in the year 1506; it was shortly afterwards visited by Tristan d'Acunha. By the Portuguese it was called the island of St. Lawrence, either in honour of its discoverer, Lawrence Almeida, or, as stated by early writers, in accordance with a custom prevailing among them, in honour of the saint on whose day in the calendar it was first seen. The French, during the reign of Henry IV., called it Isle Dauphine.

The island had, however, for a long period previously, been known to the Moors and Arabs, who have visited its western shores for the purpose of trade. By them it was called Serandah, and not Serandib, as stated by Rochon, which there is every reason to believe was the name they gave to Ceylon. The inhabitants of Europe had also been previously

---

[2] Based on the work of William Ellis.

made acquainted with its existence by the accounts of Marco Paulo, whose travels were published in the close of the 13th century. By the last mentioned traveller the island was called *Magaster*.

The word Madagascar is of uncertain import; and its use, to designate the island, appears to be of foreign rather than native origin. The inhabitants appear to be acquainted with it only as the designation .given by strangers to their country. The natives themselves have no distinct specific names for the whole of their island. By those who reside on the coast it is sometimes called Nosindambo, "island of wild hogs," from the number of these animals found in the country. In speaking of their country, the *Madegasse* usually name the several provinces respectively, or, if they have occasion to speak of the whole, some kind of periphrasis is employed, as, Izao rehetra izao, "All this entirely ;" Izao tontolo izao, " this whole ;" Ni tany rehetra, "all this country ;" or, as expressions still more emphatic, Izao ambany lanitra, "this beneath the skies;" Amhony tany ambany lanitra, "upon the earth, and beneath the skies." A familiar expression for the whole island, is, also, Ny, anivony ny riaka, signifying, literally, "The, in the midst of the flood," "that which is surrounded by water," "island." This name, however, though an appropriate term for "island," is applied by the natives to Madagascar only. The usual word for "island," in the native language, is, nosy, as, Nosy Ibrahim, "Isle of St. Mary."

The descriptions which different writers have given of Madagascar have been various, and, in many respects, dissimilar. In general, the representations of its productions, salubrity, and resources have been such as the hopes of its visitors have been led to desire, rather than such as their observations have fully authorized them to make. In the sixteenth century, the Dutch thus write: "The riches of this island are great, abounding in rice, honey, wax, cotton, lemons, cloves". The French draw a far more splendid picture. The prize, as thus announced, certainly looks tempting, but it has never yet answered the eager expectations of adventurers.

Highly coloured as the above may appear, our own countrymen have shown themselves equally capable of appreciating its Excellencies, and exhibiting its beauties and its worth.

Mr. Richard Boothby, a merchant of London, who visited Madagascar about the beginning of the seventeenth century, and published his account in 1644, after describing its soil, productions, &c., adds, "And, without all question, this country far transcends and exceeds all other countries in Asia, Africa, and America, planted by English, French, Dutch, Portuguese, and Spanish ; and it is likely to prove of far greater value and esteem to any Christian prince and nation that shall plant and settle a sure habitation therein, than the West Indies are to the king and kingdom of Spain; and it may well be compared to the land of Canaan, that flows with milk and honey ; a little world of itself, adjoining to no other land within the compass of many leagues or miles : or the chief paradise this day upon earth."

In another place, after having again spoken of its resources, he adds, "In further commendation thereof, I will take the liberty of extolling it, I hope without offence, as Moses did the land of Canaan : ' It is a good land, a land in which rivers of waters and fountains spring out of the vallies and mountains: a land of wheat and barley, of vineyards, of fig-trees and pomegranates : a land wherein thou shalt eat without scarcity, neither shalt lack any thing therein : a land whose stones are iron, and out of whose mountains thou mayest dig brass.'"

Chapter 2

General History of Madagascar[3]

I

The geological features of the country are distinct and prominent; and although hitherto but very partially examined, present considerable variety. The greater part of the island exhibits primitive formations, chiefly granite, sienite, and blocks of exceedingly pure quartz; sometimes large pieces of beautifully-coloured rose-quartz are met with; the white kind is used by the natives to ornament the summits of their tombs; cyst, intersected by broad veins of quartz, and a substance resembling grey wacke or whinstone, is frequently seen. Many of the formations are of clay-slate; and a valuable kind of slate, suitable for roofing and writing upon, has been discovered in the Betsileo country, at about a hundred miles from the capital. Silex and chert, with beautiful formations of chalcedony,

---

[3] By William Ellis.

primitive limestone, including some valuable specimens of marble, with different kinds of sandstone, are also met with. Finely-crystallized schorls frequently occur in the Betsileo country, where, embedded in limestone, apparently of fresh-water formation, specimens of fossils, including serpents, lizards, cameleons, with different kinds of vegetable fossils, have been found.

No subterranean fires are known to be at present in active or visible operation; yet in some sections of the country, especially in the Betsileo province, indications of volcanic action frequently occur, and are strongly marked. Many of the rocks, for several miles together, are composed of homogeneous earthy lava; scoria and pumice are also occasionally discovered, and some of the lavas abound with finely-formed crystals of olivine.

Besides the primitive and transition formations, and the rocks of volcanic origin, there are large beds of clay, and extensive tracts of soil composed of ferruginous earth and disintegrated lava, rich alluvial deposits, and vegetable mould. Some of the geological specimens brought home to this country are evidently carbonaceous, and would favour the expectation that there are coal formations in some parts of the island. Limestone has not yet been discovered in the eastern part of Madagascar; but coral is abundant on the coast, and furnishes the inhabitants with excellent lime.

Our acquaintance with the minerals of Madagascar, though exceedingly limited and partial, is, as far as it extends, highly satisfactory. If the diamond, and other costly gems, have not yet been discovered in its mines, and if its bowels have not yielded the precious metal by which the new world inflamed the avarice of the inhabitants of the old, and doomed its own unoffending and aboriginal occupants, first, to a merciless bondage, and, finally, to annihilation; Madagascar is already proved to be rich in the minerals most useful to man. Silver and copper have been stated by early visitors to exist in certain portions of the island: the latter is frequently visible in specimens found in the country, and brought to England; and it is still reported by the natives that the former has been obtained.

Mr. Boothby, indeed, refers to gold brought from this country: for after observing, "This gallant island of Madagascar affords these several rich commodities," which he enumerates, concluding with gold; he further states, "the old Earl of Denbigh brought home from this island of Madagascar, gold sand, which he presented to the king's majesty and the council-board; and I was at the council-board when this gold sand was in question, and approved of." Had this been correct, it is not likely that the circumstance would have been lost sight of, far more vigorous efforts would certainly have been made to discover this precious metal. The gold sand in question was, in all probability, brought from the adjacent coast of Africa.

However this may be, iron ore, a mineral to a nation in the infancy of its civilization far more valuable than gold, has been found so rich and abundant as to be rendered available to the natives, by a rude and simple process of smelting, for almost every purpose for which it is at present required. A great part of the interior district of Ankova abounds with iron. Its quality is good, but the want of coal, which has hitherto been sought for in vain, renders the smelting of it difficult. In the district of Imamo, which lies to the west of the capital, great quantities of iron ore, in a very perfect state, are found on the surface of the ground: the portion of iron is so large in some ore, as perhaps to have occasioned the remark in Rochon, a remark which is certainly not warranted by facts, that native steel is found in Madagascar. The iron in the mountain of Ambohimiangavo is so abundant, that it is called by the natives, "iron-mountain."

Rock-salt is found near the coast, and nitre has been met with; and also, abundance of pyrites, yielding a valuable per centage of sulphur. The nitre appears like hoar-frost on the surface of embankments, and other projecting parts of the ground, and is called by the people, *sira tany*, salt of the earth: it is not, however, plentiful.

II

Of native productions, used as articles of food, must be specified rice, as holding the principal place. Of the sorts cultivated in Madagascar, modern botanists have enumerated eleven varieties. The oldest people in the country agree in affirming, that this article of food, which, with the exception of the Sakalavas, may be regarded as the staff of life to the Malagasy, is of comparatively recent origin. This opinion may probably, however, refer more strictly to the introduction of rice into the interior of the island, and its cultivation there, as Flacourt gives a description of the different kinds of rice cultivated in the island before his time, nearly two hundred years ago.

The cocoa-nut is also thought to be of recent date in the island, and is supposed to have been borne by the waves from some other soil, and washed to the shores of Madagascar about one hundred and fifty years ago. The bread-fruit tree is of still more recent introduction. Plantains and bananas have been known from time immemorial.

There are also several kinds of yams, called by the natives, ovy; the manioc plant, also called manga-hazo; Indian corn, or maize, and large millet; several kinds of beans, gourds, melons, pine-apples, and earth-nuts. Lemons, oranges, citrons, limes, peaches, and mulberries also flourish luxuriantly ; some of which, it is said, were first planted by Flacourt in the south of the island. Many edible roots and vegetables grown in the neighbouring islands, at the Cape of Good Hope, and in Europe, have been introduced within the last few years, partly by the late James Hastie, esq. and Mr. Brady, and still more extensively by the members of the Mission. To the latter the island is indebted for several varieties of the Cape vine, the Cape fig, quinces, pomegranates, and, as an experiment, walnuts and almonds. Coffee has been found to succeed well.

Wheat, barley, and oats have been produced, but are not much prized by the natives, and do not seem to flourish in their soil. The European potato is extensively cultivated, and highly esteemed.

Flowers are numerous, and rare. It is, however, only during half the year that the gardens present an inviting appearance, excepting those whose low situations admit of their being watered by channels from the rivers and fountains, or other artificial means. The alternation of long seasons of heavy rain and extreme drought, are unfavourable to the culture of flowers.

Honey and wax are abundant in or near the forests, in which also are found a number of valuable gums; and not fewer than ten or twelve kinds of oil, including that of the palma-christi, are obtained from the numerous vegetable productions of the country.

With the number and peculiarities of the feathered tribes of Madagascar, we are but imperfectly acquainted; yet no field of research appears more interesting, or promises to the student in this department of the Creator's works, a more ample reward. Domestic poultry is abundant, and may be obtained at a reasonable price. Akoho is the native name for fowls, with the addition of lahy to signify the male, and vary the female. There are said to be several kinds of pheasants, called by the people, akoho-la wild akoho, or fowl of the woods; partridges are also met with, but they are smaller in size than those of Europe. The akanga, guinea-fowl, both wild and tame, is common, and found in considerable numbers.

Besides the birds which appear to be natives of the island, peacocks, turkeys, geese, and ducks, with an improved kind of fowl, have been introduced; and the latter are reared in such abundance, that numbers of them are at times sent to the Isle of France for sale. There are several kinds of pigeons in the island, and the turtle-dove, called

domohina) is found in the woods. Birds of the eagle or falcon tribe are met with in the less frequented parts of the island; crows, hawks, and kites are also seen. The screech-owl is called by the natives vorondolo, or, bird of death; lolo is the name of a disease, and, when used figuratively, signifies malice. Some writers have stated that the beautiful flamingo, called by the natives tamby, is found in Madagascar; but no one of the species has been seen by any late resident in the island. There is a large-beaked bird inhabiting the desert, called sama, but the description given of this bird does not answer to that of the splendid flamingo. Wild ducks and geese, and other water-fowl, abound in the neighbourhood of the lakes and rivers; snipes are also met with.

Though the woods and forests are peopled with several varieties of paroquets, and other tribes of splendid and beautiful plumage, but few of melody in song enliven the places of their resort. A bird of the ostrich kind is said to frequent the most desert places of the island. If a bird of this species exist in the country, the story of the ambassadors, to which Marco Paulo refers, may not be totally void of foundation.

III

Madagascar contains twenty-two chief or larger provinces. Rochon has given some account of twenty-eight, as existing in his time. It is probable that in some instances the minor divisions of a province, or even some of the principal towns, may have been reckoned as distinct and independent provinces. Most of the provinces have three or four principal divisions or districts, and these again have numerous subdivisions; as, for example, Ankova includes Imerina, Imamo, and Vonizongo, and each of these has its numerous smaller divisions. In other instances the natural division into north and south, which obtains both in the Betsileo and Sakalava countries, may have given the appearance of a greater number of independent provinces than actually existed.

The following are the provinces into which Madagascar is at present divided.

1. Vohimarina,
2. Maroa,
3. Ivongo,
4. Mahavelona,
5. Tamatave,

12. Isienimbalala,
13. Ibara,
14. Betsileo,
15. Menabe,
16. Ambongo,

6. Betanimena,
7. Anteva,
8. Matitanana,
9. Vangaidrano,
10. Anosy,
11. Androy,
17. Iboina,
18. Antsianaka,
19. Ankay,
20. Ankova,
21. Mahafaly,
22. Fiarenana.

Having given a general description of the whole island, it will not, perhaps, be deemed wholly incompatible with the avowed design of the present work, which relates principally to the interior of Madagascar, to offer a brief sketch of its several provinces. Some of the circumstances introduced, in reference to a few of the provinces, are derived from the accounts of those who have previously written on Madagascar; the others are stated as the result of information which the Missionaries themselves obtained from various quarters in the island; and the whole may be regarded as presenting, if not a perfect exhibition of the existing state of the island, yet, certainly, such a view of it as is considered correct by the best informed natives at the Capital : it is what Madagascar is at Tananarivo believed to be, and such as eye-witnesses for the most part have described it.

Vohimarina, the first, is the most northern province of the island; it is but thinly populated, and the soil, for the most part, is unproductive. The district is mountainous, and incapable of extensive cultivation. Iangogoro, one of the highest mountains in Madagascar, is situated in this province. It is sometimes called Vigarora. Its summit commands an extremely diversified and extensive prospect. There are here four principal ports : *viz.*, Diegosoray (which the natives usually call Mahazeba;) Port Luquey, or Lucas; Andravena, and Vohimarina, or, as frequently spelt, Vohimaro.

South of Vohimarina, and having Antsianaka to its west, is the province of Maroa, the second in the list already given. The general face of the country is fertile, abounding also in hills and forests. Its population, though it cannot be regarded as numerous, is far greater than that of the province last described. Some of its vegetable productions are remarkably fine;

particularly the akondro, or banana, which grows here to an extraordinary height.

Maroa readily submitted to Radama in his northern expedition of 18-23.

The most important circumstance, in connexion with the history of this province, relates to the French settlement at the bay of Antongil, which is situated here, in lat. 15°^25' S. The bay is about fourteen leagues long, from north to south, and eight broad between Cape Bellones and point Baldrick. The small islet Marotte lies about one mile from the shore. The common anchorage is to the north of Marotte, a musket-shot distance. The river bears N.N.W. from the Marotte. The anchorage off this river is called Port Choiseul.

The province of Ivong, the third, lies to the south of Maroa, and is separated from Mahavelona by the river Manangoro, which rises in a lake to the west of Antsianaka.

There is also in this province another considerable river, called Penimbala, and a port called Tahotaingia, or, as sometimes marked in maps, Teinteigne. It is generally pronounced by captains and traders at Mauritius, Tang-tang.

The general appearance of the country resembles that of Maroa, being hilly, woody, and fertile. Cattle and considerable quantities of rice are exported from this province for the markets of Bourbon and Mauritius.

The Isle of St. Mary, which occupies so prominent a place in the history of Madagascar, lies off this province, at the distance of two or three leagues, and is about forty miles N.N.E. from Foule Point. The inhabitants call themselves Zafy-Ibrahim, i.e. descendants of Abraham, and their island, Nosy-Ibrahim, Island of Abraham, The natives of the province do not generally designate themselves by this title; and it is not improbable that the name originated with some of the pirates, who were all Europeans, and who made their settlement in the Isle of St. Mary, and afterwards intermarrying with the natives, assumed the title as one of honour — one of the most innocent, perhaps, of their piratical acts.

The Isle of St. Mary's is represented as exceedingly fertile, and extends, in a northeasterly direction, from 17° 6' to 16° 37'. On the west side is a bay, having an islet called Quail's Island, at its entrance. Here small vessels may obtain shelter. The place is far from being salubrious. The French, who from time to time sent recruits to replace the troops who died in their establishment there, gave to the island the designation of "The Grave of the French." To this melancholy picture of the spot should perhaps be appended the redeeming consideration, so happily, so philanthropically suggested by the "philosophic" Rochon : — " The greatest care was taken, it is true, to send no persons thither to settle, except such as could occasion little hurt to society if they perished."

IV

From the time that Vasco de Gama in 1498 opened a passage to India by the Cape of Good Hope, numerous pirates infested those seas. They became, at length, so formidable by the success of their nefarious transactions, as to render a general effort, by the European powers interested in the Indian trade, indispensably necessary for their suppression. In the prospect of their being thus cut off from their usual resources, they formed an establishment in the Isle of St. Mary about the year 1724, and gained, by their assiduous attentions, and valuable importations, the good-will and friendship of the natives, who were ignorant of the iniquitous means by which the treasures brought to their island were obtained. They were, however, so vigorously pursued, even to their places of most secure retreat, by vessels from Europe, that their system was annihilated, and their ships burnt. After this they appear to have settled in different parts of the northern coast of Madagascar, wherever an eligible opening was presented, and connected themselves, there is every reason to believe, with the traffic in slaves, the greatest scourge ever known to the islanders, equally degrading to the inhuman trader and his hapless victims.

The next province, Mahavelona, is the fourth, which is separated from Ivongo by the Manangoro. The soil is fertile, and the country is woody, and, to some extent, brought under cultivation. It is, however, stated by the natives, that the plantations are frequently destroyed by irruptions of herds of wild hogs from the adjoining forests.

Abundance of game may be found in this district: excellent oysters are plentiful on its shores, at the head of the bay of Antongil, and especially in the bay of Ifenoarivo.

The principal trading ports in this province are, Maropototra, or Foule Pointe, and Ifenoarivo. The latter is the most valuable, and is usually called by traders from the Isle of France, Feneriffe. It is well situated for the purposes of traffic, having the advantage of water-carriage from a considerable distance in the interior. By this means, rice, yams, and other vegetables are conveyed to the coast with greater despatch and facility, and at a less expense, than in most other ports.

Foule Pointe, called also Marofototra (names of the same signification — the former, French, the latter, Malagasy,) is important for trade on its own account, and is a desirable station for traders, on account also of its contiguity to Tamatave, Ifenoarivo, Antongil bay, and St. Mary's. The two principal rivers in Mahavelona are, Ony-be, and Ifontsy, which divides it from Tamatave.

The province of Mahaviilona is considered as highly insalubrious. Many of the troops sent to Foule Point by Radama, in 1823, were seized with fever, and the forces of the sovereign so reduced by its prevalence, that not long afterwards Itasy, a native chieftain, raised the standard of rebellion. He was, however, taken prisoner in 1827, and conducted to the capital, Tananarivo, where he still remains under guard.

A number of Arabs, as well as French traders from Mauritius and Bourbon, have settlements in this part of the country. The Arabs have, in fact, established themselves along the whole eastern coast of Madagascar.

Tamatave, the fifth, is the next province, and lies to the south of Mahavelona. Its principal town or port on the coast, takes the name of the district itself, which Europeans call Tamatave, or Tamatavy, but by the natives it is universally called Taomasina.

The port of Tamatave is one of the finest on the eastern coast of the island. The adjoining reefs are extensive, and the swell and surf heavy and appalling, but they are considered dangerous only to vessels entering or leaving when the wind blows strong from the northeast.

Tamatave is a small and irregularly-built village, situated on a low point of land, with an anchorage in about nine fathoms water within the coral reef. Its latitude is 18°12" south. There are about two hundred houses in the village, and from eight hundred to a thousand inhabitants. The habitations of the natives are of very inferior construction; those belonging to European and Creole traders are better; and a few are comfortable and substantial. The Hovas erected a battery at the northern extremity of the village: being, however, merely an enclosure formed of strong poles, and containing three or four native houses belonging to the government, together with a powder-magazine and several smaller tenements, the whole was destroyed by the French in their attack on the island, in 1829.

Another battery, built of coral, has been subsequently erected near the spot, and planted with a few pieces of cannon.

The materials employed in the construction of the houses in Tamatave are the ravin-ala, or traveller's-tree, the rofia, and bamboo; the roofs are composed of the leaves

of the traveller's-tree, which soon decay. The houses consist of but one room, though this is sometimes divided by a fragile partition of matting. The floor is of flattened bamboos fastened to poles, which are raised in order to avoid the dampness, that would otherwise be equally unpleasant and injurious.

The principal exports from Tamatave consist in rice, poultry, bullocks, and rofia cloth; and several vessels are employed in the trade between this port and Mauritius.

Some also visit it from Bourbon, for the same purposes. The neighbourhood is extremely damp and swampy; and, as may be supposed, the village and its vicinity are at all times far from being salubrious; but the most unhealthy period is from the middle of November to the beginning of March. The freshness and luxuriance of the verdure give so delightful an appearance to the scenery, that a stranger can scarcely regard it as the seat of disease; but a few days' residence makes him sensible of the constant exhalations from the marshes, which are so productive of the justly dreaded fever of the coast.

The country is woody and marshy, A considerable quantity of rice is cultivated here, called the tavy, which is grown, not on the low ground, where it may be constantly covered with water, but on high ground, frequently the side of a hill. The culture of the rice is extremely simple. The trees are cut down, and, after burning the stumps, the rice-seed is planted in the spot, covered with the ashes, and with but little subsequent care the crop is generally abundant.

In the interior of this province is the fine lake of *Nosivé*, one of the most extensive in the island. This lake is from twenty to twenty-five miles in length. It contains several small islands, some of which are inhabited. It forms part of the series of lakes already noticed, and which are known to reach upwards of two hundred miles on the eastern coast of Madagascar.

Eight or nine miles from Tamatave, is the village of Anjolokefa, occasionally called Hivondrona, (and in some maps marked Ivondro,) though Hivondrona is more properly the name of the river only, which proceeding from the interior of the country, falls into the sea at the distance of about two hundred yards from the village.

Anjolokefa was the residence of the enterprising chieftain Fisatra, otherwise called

Fische, or Fish. He held in subjection to himself all the inhabitants of the Betanimena,

Tamatave, and Mahavelona provinces. This village was at that time the principal place on the coast. His very name was a terror even through the province of Ankay, (west of Betanimena,) the eastern part of which he conquered. He was at length murdered by a party from the interior, who contemplated in his death the ruin also of his brother and ally, John Rene, of Tamatave. In this they failed: John Rene lived to inflict terrible vengeance on the murderers of his relative. A son of Fisatra, named Berora, intended to succeed to his father's possessions, was placed for some time under the care of the Rev. D. Jones, on the commencement of the missionary efforts of the latter at

Tamatave, but was shortly afterwards taken from the island, and conveyed to Paris for education, where he lately died.

What political views the French government may have had in this measure, remain yet to be developed in the future connexions France may form with Madagascar.

To the west of Hivondrona is a fine cataract called Ifito; inferior, however, to some in the Betanimena country; and in the division called Ivoloina, there are two immense caverns.

Betanimena, the sixth, is the province adjoining Tamatave to the south, separated from it by Tany-fotsy, and stretching about thirty-five leagues along the coast. The name of the province signifies "much red earth," and, no doubt was given from the reddish ferruginous appearance of the soil. There are several extensive lakes in this district, and two cataracts, Tahaviara, and landrianahomby, deserving the notice of travelers. The country is flat near the sea, hilly in the interior, and mountainous towards the north. It is in many parts marshy, and covered with thickets and forests. The soil for some distance from the coast is sandy; but for the most part productive, from the abundance of decomposed vegetable matter which it contains. The population is numerous. At Ambohibohazo, the capital of the province, the soil is rich, and the scenery diversified and beautiful.

In the neighbourhood of Ambohibohazo, Mr. Hastie selected a spot of ground for a plantation of mulberries. They succeed well, and might be cultivated to an indefinite extent for silkworms. Some good silk has already been produced in Madagascar; and this valuable commodity may hereafter become an article of great importance to the island. Mr. Hastie intended to form a sugar plantation in the same neighbourhood, for which the soil appeared well adapted. Labour being extremely cheap, there was every prospect that the establishment would have succeeded. But his lamented decease, and subsequently that of Radama, have suspended every plan of the kind then in contemplation, and have shewn, most distinctly, the extent and beneficial influence each exerted over the people, while they exhibit in an affecting light the degree to which a single individual may promote, or his removal retard, the improvement of a nation.

There is abundance of grazing-land in the same part of the province; and numerous herds of cattle, belonging to the sovereign, and to the traders on the coast, are usually taken there for some time previously to their exportation. It is also from this part of the country that "maromita," usually called by Europeans "marmittes," (coolies or earers,) are generally obtained, for conveying travelers and their luggage, or merchandise, from the coast to the capital, or other parts of the interior.

This district has also been famous for its *jiolahy*, or brigands. They have concealed themselves in the recesses of its almost impenetrable forests and thickets, or extensive and generally unknown caverns; whence suddenly rushing forth on passengers and bearers of burdens, they have committed with impunity extensive depredations, not unfrequently adding murder to their robberies.

Vatomandry is a small port in this province, but has scarcely any trade. At Tany-fotsy an important junction between two extensive lakes was commenced by Radama, in order to facilitate communications with the interior by means of water-carriage.

Anteva the seventh province, lies to the south of Betanimena, which it resembles in general appearance, though it is rather more hilly. Rice is grown in this province in great abundance, and quantities of beef are salted here for exportation, though the inhabitants are extremely poor.

The great cause of the poverty of this part of the island, is, the love of ardent spirits prevalent among the people. After toiling to obtain a crop of rice, the natives will sometimes sell the whole for a small quantity of arrack, imported by traders from Mauritius and Bourbon. With the deleterious drug thus heartlessly given in return for the produce of their labour, the natives soon become intoxicated, in which humiliating state they continue so long as the arrack lasts: for this short-lived indulgence, they sink into a state of the most abject penury and misery, and then force themselves and their families to subsist the greater part of the year on roots, &c. found in the woods and swamps.

Their chief means of subsistence is the via, a species of arum, the root of which is tuberous or cylindrical, and frequently from ten to twelve inches in diameter. It is dressed by baking for about twelve hours in an oven of heated stones underground, after the manner of the South Sea islanders. In this state it will keep good for three or four days, but is cut into small pieces and dried in the sun, when intended to be kept for a longer period.

In payment for the carriage of goods into the interior, or for their produce, the intoxicating draught is the usual equivalent: to diminish, and if possible prevent, the wretchedness thus induced, Radama imposed a heavy duty on the importation of ardent spirits. Some check on such an improvident and destructive infatuation in the one party, and of relentless avarice in the other, was required; but there is great reason to fear that the baneful habit is too deeply fixed among the unthinking natives of this part of the coast, to be very easily extirpated; but the attempt of Radama to diminish the evil, is only one among many instances of the soundness of his judgment and the beneficial tendency of his measures. There are three important ports in this province: Manoro, Mahela, and Mananjary. A considerable trade is carried on at these places, especially at Mananjary, by French settlers.

The eighth, the province of Matitanana, lies south of Anteva, and has for a length of time been the principal settlement of the Arabs, on the east coast of Madagascar.

Matitanana is also famous for a class of persons called by some writers Ombiasses, but more correctly Mpiasa, which signifies "workers." They appear to resemble the Mpisikidy, Mpanandro, and Mpanao-ody of the interior, whose profession is to work the sikidy, or divination, to calculate days, foretell fortunes, as well as to prepare medicines and charms. It has been conjectured that most of the superstitions in the island have had their origin in this province.

Madagascar is the land of ody, or charms, and in this district they triumph in all their melancholy glory. The country in general is flat, but fertile; rice, sugarcane, and cattle abound.

Vangaidrano, the ninth, or as sometimes called, Taisaka, joins the south of Matitanana. Here very little advancement has yet been made, or even attempted in civilization, yet the population is considerable.

The Manabatra with seven mouths, and the Mantangy with four, are the two principal rivers in this province. The Malagasy fever, which prevails more or less along the whole coast of the island, is very general, and to strangers often fatal, on the coast of this province. The country is flat and marshy. There are also extensive and almost impervious forests, where vegetation is rank, and the free circulation of the air intercepted by thick underwood. The productions are much the same as in the provinces already described, though little is attempted by the natives beyond the cultivation of a supply adequate to their immediate wants.

Anosy, the tenth, is south of Vangaidrano, and on some accounts is one of the most important provinces, in the history of

Madagascar. It has been the site of the most extensive French establishments; and the principal efforts of the Catholic missionaries in Madagascar have been put forth here. In Anosy also is situated the most fertile and

beautiful vale in the island, the vale of Ambolo. The country is populous, and the soil extremely fertile. Rice and manioc, sugarcane and coffee, are abundant. Its extensive marshes render it, however, like the greater part of the lower portions of the island, extremely insalubrious.

There are in this province several rivers, and in the northern part of Anosy is the bay of St. Lucia, called by the natives Mangafiafy. Ten leagues south of St. Lucia, is the peninsula in which Fort Dauphin stands; the earliest French settlement in the island. The peninsula is called Taolanara, or, as sometimes written, Tholangari.

Fort Dauphin is in lat. 25°5' S. and long. 46°35' E. The shores are often bold and steep; and the cliffs appear composed of strata of limestone, of varied thicknesses. Rock-salt and saltpetre are found in this province. In fact, next to the Betsileo country, of which we shall have occasion to speak presently, Anosy may be considered the finest province in the island — the most beautiful and the most productive. Of the rich vale of Ambolo, mention has been already made. In this charming valley, not only the usual produce of the island, but cloves and other spices, with citrons of various kinds, may be obtained. Hot springs, reported to possess valuable medicinal qualities, are also found there. It was, perhaps, from this fertile spot, that Monsieur de Modave drew materials for his too flattering memoirs of the island of Madagascar.

The next province is the eleventh, Androy separated by the river Mahafaly from Anosy. Of this and the adjoining provinces, (twenty-first and twenty-second,) Mahafaly and Fiarenana, there is, perhaps, little to be said. Scarcely any advancement has been made in the civilization of their inhabitants, excepting in this one important circumstance, that the chiefs of the two latter provinces, in voluntarily submitting to Radama, agreed to his propositions on the subject of the suppression of the slave-trade in Madagascar. The country is woody, and the population small. Wild cattle abound. Salt and nitre are found in Mahafaly and Fiarenana. Tolia Bay and St. Augustine Bay are situated in the province of Fiarenana; it is to this part of the country that Drury's notice of Madagascar principally refers; and there also the Winterton was lost in August 1792. The ship was wrecked in the district of the bay of St. Augustine, about fifteen or twenty miles from Tolia. The soil in the neighbourhood of Toha is sandy and unproductive, but improving towards the bay of St. Augustine.

Before proceeding to the next great division of the western coast, it may be proper to remark, that there are two inland provinces lying between Mahafaly and Fiarenana on the west, and Anosy on the east: — the twelfth, called Tsienimhalala; and the thirteenth, Ibara; the former to the south, bordering on Androy; the latter to the north, joining the Betsileo country. Of these, however, little more can be said than respecting the western provinces, to which they are contiguous. They have never been carefully explored, either by natives or foreigners. It is known that they are but thinly peopled. The country is woody, and a very inconsiderable portion of it is brought under cultivation. The inhabitants have obtained from the adjoining maritime provinces, supplies of arms and ammunition, and their acknowledgment of the sovereignty of the Plovas appears the effect of compulsion rather than of cordiality. They possess great numbers of cattle, which they dispose of on the coast, in exchange for ammunition and arms.

Immediately to the north of Ibara, is the province of Betsileo — the fourteenth. The name signifies "much, not conquered," or "invincible," and denotes the independent and unconquered spirit of the inhabitants. It is separated from Ankova by a range of mountains called Ankaratra, and from Anteva by an extensive waste or desert. Betsileo is a fine grazing country. The cattle are exceedingly numerous, and among them some are found, called "omby bory," cattle without horns. The account given by some authors, of cattle in Madagascar having horns appended to the forehead by means of a small portion of skin, appears fabulous. Such cattle are not now known in the island, and it is believed never were.

The inhabitants of the Betsileo province, though not equally advanced in civilization with the people of Ankova, who have had more intercourse with Europeans, are remarkable for the mildness of their dispositions, and the simplicity of their manners. Living in an inland province, and having had scarcely any communication with strangers visiting the island or setthng on the coast, they naturally express the utmost surprise at the appearance, manners, and pursuits of the foreigners, when they meet with any of these, to them, singular and extraordinary beings.

Generally speaking, the Betsileo lead an inactive life.

The principal domestic occupation of the people consists in the manufacture of the native lamba, or long robe, from a kind of coarse silk, the produce of the country, which they render extremely heavy by ornamenting with an immense quantity of small leaden beads fastened to the silk in rows either straight or curved. They purchase the metal on the coast, or in the interior, and make the beads themselves. Their land is fertile, and, with but trifling labour, yields an ample supply for the few wants with which they are familiar; and to exert themselves beyond this, in their present grade of civilization, would be contrary to the known laws and history of the human species.

Betsileo is divided into six districts, — three in the north, and an equal number in the south. The former, which are situated nearly in the centre of the island, are Andrasay, or Vakinankaratra, Fisakanana, and Vohidrahomby. To the south, are Lalongina, Sandrabe, and Tsianipariha. The scenery of the country is not unfrequently rich and varied, occasionally it is picturesque, and sometimes bold and majestic; and the indications of former volcanic action are distinct and numerous.

To the west of Betsileo, and proceeding northward on the sea-coast, is the fifteenth province, the large country of Menabe, otherwise designated the South Sakalava country. This district has from time immemorial been renowned for the brave and warlike chieftains by whom its inhabitants have been governed.

The prevalence of wars in former times, among the Sakalavas, together with the fatal effects of the fever abounding in this district, may sufficiently account for the fact, that, though the aggregate population is considerable, it is yet small compared with the amount the Sakalava country is capable of maintaining. The cultivated part of the province is large; other portions yet remain desert.

Various esculent roots are cultivated by the Sakalavas, especially arrow-root. The tamarind is abundant, and several fruits but little known in the island. Cattle, though still abundant, are not so numerous as formerly, owing chiefly to the destructive and predatory nature of their wars.

On the borders of this province, between Menabe and Ankova, is a large tract of country occupied by herds of cattle in the wild state; many of them are distinguished from other cattle in Madagascar, by not having the "tafona," or hump on the back. To hunt these animals, was a favourite amusement of Radama. The spot usually chosen for the feat, is called Manerinerina.

The fine and extensive vale of Belisa is situated in this province, running in a direction north and south. It is watered by three considerable rivers, the Imania, the Manambolo, and the Manambala. There is also an extensive lake of the same name as the first river mentioned, Imania, famed for having near its centre a beautiful and picturesque islet called Anosisaka. This is adorned with a remarkably fine natural grove, rendering it an attractive object, in the scenery of which it is so distinguished an ornament.

North of the Sakalava country is, sixteenth, Amhongo having a considerable extent of sea-coast, and being for the most part, a level and woody district. The country resembles that of the Sakalavas, but its inhabitants are less civilized; they may, perhaps, be termed barbarous. In more than one instance, cruelty has been shown to foreigners who have been unfortunately shipwrecked on this part of the coast. A case of this kind occurred a few years ago, when a Portuguese whaler being cast on this part of the island, the crew were all murdered.

Ambongo is the only province in Madagascar, whose inhabitants did not, more or less, acknowledge the sovereignty of Radama, and whom he had not attempted to reduce to subjection.

The principal rivers here are, the Manambaho, the Sambaho, and lantsanira, which last falls into the sea south of Cape St. Andrew. The province is separated from Iboina by the river Mangaray.

Seventeenth, Iboina lies north of Ambongo. This province is also level and woody. It abounds in marshes, and hence also in fevers. The population is considerable, and the soil is generally productive. Cattle is very numerous. The chief river here is the Betsiboka, which runs into the sea near Mojanga. Near this is the small village of Bombitoka. This name seems to be a corruption of the Malagasy Vohirn-be toaka, i.e. "the village of much spirituous liquor." The Arabs have long been accustomed to visit this place, and many of them reside here for the purposes of trade; they are called by the Malagasy, Talaotra.

To the east of Iboina lies Vohimarina, which has been already described. The Betsileo country has been spoken of as south of Ankova; that to the north, the eighteenth province, is called Antsianaka." This is an extensive tract of country, abounding with large herds of cattle.

Sheep, as well as bullocks, are numerous here. Rice is not largely cultivated, but the finest cotton in the island is produced in this province, and its cultivation might be greatly increased, as the soil appears well adapted to its growth. Great quantities are sold in the markets in the raw state, and afterwards manufactured by the natives into dresses. Their process is slow and tedious, but the cloth manufactured is firm and durable. The country, though large, is not populous, and is also far from being healthy; a Malagasy fever prevails extensively. The houses are mere huts, and generally excessively dirty. Very little has yet been attempted for the civilization or mprovement of the inhabitants of this part of the island.

The high road toTananarivo from Mahavelona, in which Foule Pointe is situated, lies through the province of Antsianaka. The province is intersected by a part of the great forest of Alamazaotra. There is also a beautiful lake in this province, called Anosy, having an island in its centre, and a village occupying the highest part of the island.

The province of Ankay the nineteenth, lies to the south of Antsianaka, and to the west of Ankova. It is a narrow strip of the interior of the country, and is sometimes called Antankay. Its inhabitants are called Bezanozano ; a people of independent spirit, and formerly among the most turbulent and anarchical in the island; anarchical is, in fact, the signification of the name Bezanozano. The inhabitants are not numerous, and the villages are small. Cattle and poultry are abundant ; rice is largely cultivated. The people are, however, generally poor and dirty, and much addicted to divination and idols. The dialect spoken, like that of Antsianaka, being strongly nasal, resembles that of the coast more than that of the adjoining inland province of Ankova.

The scenery of many parts of Ankay is extremely beautiful and picturesque. The province consists principally of an extensive plain, situated between lofty hills, and watered by the fine river Mangoro, which runs eastward to Anteva.

West of this river is a mountain called Ifody, covered for the most part with a forest: it commands an extensive view of the country north and south. A beautiful wood resembling mahogany, called mango wood, and excellent for cabinet work, is found here, though not known to exist elsewhere in the island. The river Mangoro, from its

direction and magnitude, would be well adapted for the conveyance of merchandise between the coast and the interior of the island, but for its numerous and rapid falls, which in some places may be considered cataracts ; and, though not so large as to deserve notice as objects of curiosity or surprise, render the currents too impetuous for the purposes of navigation.

The only province remaining to be noticed is Ankova. But as this province is the country of the present rulers of the island, the site of the capital, the seat of the government, as well as having been the principal and almost exclusive scene of the labours of the Protestant Mission in the island, a more detailed account is required of this central part of the island.

Chapter III

Population of Madagascar

Madagascar is not inhabited by one single race (presenting only minor and provincial differences, yet having a common origin, and constituting an extended nation), but by a number of distinct tribes, more or less numerous, evidently derived from more than one source; differing also in many respects from each other; and remaining, at the present time, though nominally comprised in one political empire, distinct and peculiar nations. No single account would, therefore, present a just description of the various tribes comprised in the population of Madagascar.

There are, however, points in which they bear a general resemblance to each other; among these are the following : the inhabitants are rather below the middle stature, which but few exceed ; and their countenances do not exhibit that prominency of features which so frequently distinguishes the European and Asiatic nations. The men are more elegantly formed than the women, in whom there is usually a greater tendency to corpulency than in the other sex.

The beards of the men are but weak, and are plucked out in youth. Their hands are not so warm to the touch as those of Europeans, and their blood by thermometer is colder. These appear the chief among the few points in which, physically considered, there is any resemblance between the several nations. The distinction most strongly marked is that of colour; and this, though presenting slight variations in each tribe, separates the population of Madagascar into two great classes, and is by some supposed to allow of its being traced to only two sources — the one distinguished by a light, exquisitely formed person, fair complexion, and straight or curling hair; the other more robust, and dark-coloured, with woolly hair. In one or the other of these classes, the several tribes inhabiting the island may be included.

The accompanying wood- cut of the likeness of the chief officer in the embassy sent to England and France in 1835, which is copied from an excellent portrait taken by Sperling, is given as exhibiting the characteristics of the fair or olive-coloured class.

With regard simply to colour, there are but two distinct races in Madagascar — the olive and the black. But as these have occasionally intermixed, there are all possible varieties between them; and in some it would be difficult to affirm to which division they belonged, being as much inclined to one colour as the other. The vigour of health frequently gives a ruddy tinge to the countenance of the olive-coloured race; but this, while it removes them from approximating in complexion to the yellow hue of the

Malays, does not give them any resemblance to the copper-coloured Indians of America.

With respect to the quality of the hair, there are two divisions also — the Tsotra, (tso-bolo,) straight, and the Ngita, curly, or rather, frizzly. These have also inter-mixed; and the same remark applies here as to colour — the frizzly has become almost straight in some cases, and the straight almost frizzly.

The above two distinctions of colour and hair do not, however, make two separate classes, but rather four; for there are: — 1). olive-coloured natives having straight hair; and, 2). olive-coloured natives with curly or frizzly hair : of this class the accompanying Avood-cut of one of the members of the late embassy to Europe is given as an illustration. Besides the two classes just described, there are, 3). blacks having straight hair, and, 4). blacks with curly or frizzly hair. But, ordinarily, the straight hair is with the olive-coloured; and the curly or frizzly, with the black.

Besides the distinctions arising from colour and hair, which would exhibit the people in two great classes, the olive and the black, the population of the island may be considered as comprised in four chief or principal political divisions, occupying as many large geographical sections, which are also in a certain sense identical; as the designation of the people and the country they inhabit is frequently the same. These divisions are, first, the Hova; second, the Sakalava ; third, the

Betsileo; fourth, the Betanimena and Betsimisaraka.

In the early part of the reign of the father of the late Radama, a period not more than seventy years ago, the Malagasy were divided into not fewer than fifty distinct tribes, governed by their respective chieftains, and independent of each other; the chief of each tribe exercising absolute power over the lives, property, and services of his subjects. Since that period the processes of amalgamation have been rapid and effectual, and the principal divisions now recognized are those already named: all the rest are either subdivisions of these, or people belonging to one or the other intermixed. That they are all nearly the same, is manifest from their general colour, language, customs, and the names of towns, rivers, hills, and productions.

That they are in some measure also distinct tribes, is manifest from their dialects, and some peculiar customs. That they have intermingled, is manifest from their intestine wars, which have not been extirminating wars, nor wars prosecuted wholly for obtaining slaves for exportation, but wars of conquest, booty, and domestic slavery.

They have been in the habit also of wandering or fleeing from one part of the country to another, when pursued by an enemy more powerful than themselves, and settling where there was the greatest prospect of safety, just as the remains of the Vazimba, the original inhabitants of Ankova, now reside between the Imania and the Imanambolo, in Menabe. A greater approximation to general amalgamation will be perceived in the course of a few years, from the constant residence of the Hova troops at distant parts, in military stations on different parts of the island, as most of these troops either intermarry with the women of the provinces, or live with them in a far less honourable state. The chief divisions, already referred to, we now proceed to notice; both as they regard the people themselves, and the portions of the country they respectively occupy.

Geographically considered, the Sakalavas, with whom we commence, are divided into two great sections. North and South Sakalavas : the first includes the inhabitants of

Iboina in the north, and Ambongo in the north-west; the latter, those of Menabe in the west and south-west, extending on the west side of the island to Firenenana, which continues to the south of St. Augustine's Bay. This extensive region is sometimes called the Sakalava country.

A mixture of the Sakalavas and Betsileo inhabit the regions to the south of Firenenana, embracing the southern extremity of the island.

By some the Bezanozano, a small tribe, chiefly inhabiting Ankay, situated on the southeast of Ankova, are considered as a branch of the Sakalavas. The Antsianaka, inhabiting the province of the same name, to the north of Ankova, are also considered as belonging to this nation, which includes the black races of Madagascar.

The Bezanozano and Antsianaka, are supposed to have been conquered, and first separated, in a state of captivity, or driven by war from the other Sakalavas, though the distance to which they are removed is not great : the Bezanozano, on the east, (occupying Ankaratra,) may be supposed to have descended from the northern Sakalavas, occupying Iboina, &c., and the Bezanozano on the north-west, have probably descended from the Sakalavas of Ambongo or Menabe.

The next division of the country, according to the races of the people, is the Betsileo, lying immediately within that of the southern Sakalavas, and comprehending the interior or central provinces of the island. It extends from Ankaratra southward, through Tatsimo to Tanosy; Tatsimo being another name for "southern Betsileo." The Tanosy seem to be a branch of the southern Betsileo, blended with the Betanimena, whose country proceeds from the southern extremity along the eastern side of the island, and stretches to Anteva, the province bordering on the country of the Batanimena and the Bezanozano.

The country of the Betsileo also includes rather less of the north part of the island than formerly. The region immediately beyond the Ankaratra range of hills to the south, sometimes called the Betsileo country, probably belonged to the latter before they were subdued by the Hovas, nearly forty years ago. But the country to the south, nearest the Ankaratra, is now reckoned a part of Ankova, and is called Vakinankaratra, i e. "broken off by Ankaratra," and this proceeds south to the Imania; but from the Imania southward, to a limit not very accurately defined, the country is called Betsileo. Beyond this boundary it is called Tatsimo, or southern Betsileo, and though Vakinankaratra is now one of the six divisions of Ankova, its inhabitants are evidently Betsileo, who are spread over an extent of country greatly exceeding that of the province which bears their name. The Betsileo are evidently one of the most ancient races in the island, and, according to their own traditions, came originally from Anteva, a province on the south-western coast, and now inhabited by the mixed race of the Betanimena and Betsimisaraka.

The country of the Betanimena commences southward at the Mananjary, and terminates northward at Tany-fotsy : the country of the

Betsimisaraka spreads along the eastern shore till it joins that of the Sakalavas of the north, which includes the country sometimes called Hiarambazaha, or Vohimaro.

An account of Ankova, the country of the Hovas, has been formerly given, and those of the other chief divisions of the island have been added; it will, therefore, be proper

to give some account of the nations or races by whom they are severally inhabited.

The first and most important race is the Hovas, who inhabit the province of Ankova. They have in every respect the pre-eminence, and possess the entire sovereignty over the greater number of the other provinces.

From Ankova, and from Vakinankaratra, the army of Radama, by which the greater part of the island was conquered, and by which the conquest is maintained, was exclusively formed; and the island may, therefore, be regarded as held in subjection by the Hovas. The army was, in the first instance, formed at Tananarivo, the capital of the Hovas, and afterwards augmented from other parts of the province.

The use of the word Hova, though generally employed to designate the olive-coloured race, requires further explanation : — First, as to Ankova, or the country of the Hovas. This is the principal residence of the olive-coloured race, and as they seem to be the proper and original Hovas, they give name to the district where they reside. But these olive-coloured are not the only inhabitants of Ankova. There are quite as many who are black, but who are also called Hovas, from their residing in Ankova; in fact, there are comparatively few who are not black residing out of Imerina, and Imerina forms only one division of Ankova; and in Imamo, Mandridrano, Vonizongo, Valalafotsy, and Vakinankaratra, a large majority are black. Yet, in a restricted sense, all these, as belonging to Ankova, may be called Hovas. Hence, then, the race of the Hovas (olive-coloured) resides in Ankova, and gives name to the district. But all are not olive-coloured Hovas who reside in Ankova, for there are black natives also who are Hovas. So that in one sense, all are Hovas that live in Ankova — that is, so far as the name of a district is concerned. But in another sense, all are not Hovas that live in Ankova — that is, so far as a difference of origin prevails.

Another signification of the term is, perhaps, the most important: the Hovas are a race distinct from all the rest of the natives of Madagascar, an olive-coloured race, and evidently not the aborigines of the country; whether they are of Malay origin, or of an African kingdom north of Mosambique, (as was thought by Prince Coroller,) or from Abyssinia, as the same prince at one time supposed, are matters for inquiry and speculation. There is, perhaps, considerable reason for thinking that the Hova race may be a colony of Javanese; but to detail the circumstances on which that opinion has been founded, might be thought tedious and uniteresting.

If a stranger were to land on the coast, say, at Tamatave, and meet an olive-coloured native, he would be quite safe in saying, "This is a Hova," as to his physical race and origin. But as that same Hova might happen also to be a nobleman, it would be an affront to call him a

Hova, for he must be called an Andriana. Or, he might chance to be a slave, and then it would be a title of too much honour to call him Hova.

The central province of Madagascar is now the country of the Hovas. They are not, however, the aborigines of this part of the country, and it is impossible to determine, with certainty, from what part of the island they came, and obtained possession of this region. It is, however, their general belief, that they came from the south-east of Madagascar, and gradually dispossessed the aborigines of the country.

There is some ground for supposing the Vazimba were the first inhabitants of Ankova. The term Vazimba has three several significations. In its strictest sense, it appears to express the aborigines of the interior of the island of Madagascar, from whatever part of the coast they may have come. In a former part of this chapter, it has been mentioned that between the two famous rivers, Imania and Imanambolo, in Menabe, there exists a small race of people called Vazimba, and it has been at times thought, that they exhibit some correspondence with the accounts given by Rochon, of a people called the Kimos, inhabiting the interior of the island. The notices given by Rochon are far too long for insertion here, but the amount of them is briefly this, "That in the interior of Madagascar is a nation of dwarfs, averaging three feet six inches in stature, called Kimos, (or Quimos,) that they are of a lighter colour than the negroes; their hair short and woolly, that their arms are unusually long, that their females generally nourish their young with cow's milk; that in intellectual faculties they are equal to other inhabitants of the island ; that they are active, industrious, and courageous; that they manufacture iron and steel, of which they make lances and assagays ; that they have villages on the summits of high mountains, live chiefly on vegetables, and rear great quantities of cattle; that they hold no communication with the other islanders, and are perfectly peaceable, unless provoked and attacked." The writer adds, "that at the distance of two or three days' journey from Fort Dauphin are several small barrows or hillocks, owing their origin to a former massacre of these Kimos."

Singular as this account is, particularly in the instance of the diminutive stature of the people described, it is confidently reported, that on the banks of the rivers already named, there still exists a race of natives corresponding generally with the particulars stated by Rochon. The distance, however, of these rivers from Fort Dauphin is considerably greater than the situation mentioned by Rochon as the country of this nation of dwarfs. He speaks of sixty leagues north-west of Fort Dauphin, and west of Matitany. The distance to the rivers in Menabe must be, according to any calculation approaching to accuracy, 100 or 120 leagues. The people may, however, have migrated farther north within the last century; or, what is still more probable, Rochon's account may have been incorrect.

Flacourt treats the subject in a very brief and cavalier-like style, regarding the whole account as fabulous, and forming merely an amusing counterpart to the stories of the giants. Rochon condemns the incredulity of Flacourt, and thinks he has solid facts to oppose to his scepticism on the point. The most objectionable part of the account respects the stature; in this there must be a mistake, nearly all the rest is credible. A few dwarfs are met with in Imerina, but probably not in any greater proportion to the population than in other countries, and certainly not in sufficient numbers, nor possessing any peculiarities of form, to justify a belief of their having constituted a distinct race.

It is observable, that the traditional account given in the present day, of the Vazimba, is, that they formed a race of people a little below the common stature, having a remarkably thin and flat configuration of the head, and narrowing to the forehead. Their graves correspond with the description given by Rochon. They resemble small barrows, or gentle elevations of earth, with an upright stone placed in or near the centre, and a number of smaller stones rudely thrown together, like the ruins of an ancient grave.

It is not easy to arrive at any distinct conclusion: possibly the Vazimba, said to have lived formerly in Imerina, and whose graves still exist, came originally from the same part of the country as those who are now said to occupy the banks of the two rivers in Menabe, and that these may be a part of the people described by M.M. de Modave, de Commerson, and de Surville, in the "Voyage de Rochon." Their accounts are, perhaps, exaggerated, yet not without some foundation in truth. It is, however, somewhat remarkable, that many of the particulars stated by the above writers, exactly correspond with the Hovab, excepting the diminutive stature. The Hovas are certainly below the general stature of the Malagasy, and this may easily have given rise to the report of their "pygmean" dimensions. But in regard to colour, intelligence, activity, industry, courage, manufactures, productions, habitations, the Hovas are what Rochon describes the Kimos to be.

Without entering further into the inquiry at present, it may be sufficient to remark, that tradition and a few incidental circumstances induce the belief that the first settlers in Imerina came from some part eastward of Tananarivo, and fixed their residence at the villages of Alasora, Ambohitraina, and the neighbourhood. These villages are within a few miles of the capital, and they are unquestionably among the most ancient in that part of the country.

They, as well as most places in Imerina, contain numerous graves of the Vazimba; constituting, as will be afterwards shewn, the sacred places at which the natives offer their religious worship. One circumstance indicating, agreeably to the customs of the country, the antiquity and early importance of Ambohitraina, is, that its speakers, to the present day, are renowned in the public kabarys, i.e. assemblies of the people, for tracing to a remote antiquity the genealogy and origin of their chieftains; a circumstance to which the Malagasy attach the highest importance.

The population of Ankova is variously estimated; but, probably, taking an average from the conflicting statements given, from eighty to one hundred thousand may be regarded as nearly correct. This population is widely scattered in numerous villages over the surface of the country.

The villages usually contain from fifty to one hundred houses each; while the capital, with its immediate vicinity, contains a much larger number of inhabitants than any other equal portion of the country. Most of the villages are situated on eminences; some of them are extremely high, and difficult of access. They are usually encircled, for security, by a deep fosse; the earth from which being thrown up on the inner side, forms a bank round the village, which renders it difficult to scale the sides of the ditch, and adds to the safety of the people.

The language of Ankova may be considered as the standard of the Madagascar dialects. It is also the most copious, and, being the least nasal, is the most pleasing to the ear of an European. Its copiousness may in part be accounted for by the constant influx of strangers from all parts of the island; these strangers, as well as the soldiers returning from the different provinces after a campaign, or a season of garrison duty, bring with them in many cases, no doubt without being aware of it, or intending it, valuable additions to the stock of the Tenin-kova, the language of the Hovas.

In person, as already remarked, the Hovas are generally below the middle stature. Their complexion is a light olive, frequently fairer than that of the inhabitants of the southern parts of Europe; their features rather flat than prominent; their lips occasionally thick and projecting, but often thin, and the lower gently projecting, as in the Caucasian race: their hair is black, but soft, fine, and straight, or curling; their eyes are hazel, their figure erect; and though inferior in size to some of the other tribes, they are well proportioned. Their limbs are small, but finely-formed; and their gait and movements are agile, free, and graceful. Though distinguished by their promptitude and activity, their strength is inferior to that of other tribes; and they are far more susceptible of fatigue from travelling or labour.

Next to the Hovas are the Sakalavas. More numerous, especially when regarded as comprehending the Bezanozano and the Antsianaka, than their successful rivals, and occupying more extensive territories, this nation was, during the last century, the most powerful in Madagascar, having reduced the Hovas to subjection, and exacted from them a formal acknowledgment of their dependence. Tribute was annually sent from Ankova to the king of Menabe, the ruler of the South Sakalavas, until Radama invaded their territories with an army of one hundred thousand men, and induced their chieftain to form with him a treaty of peace. The Sakalavas are a brave and generous people; physically considered, they are the finest race in Madagascar. In person they are tall and robust, but not corpulent; their limbs are well formed, muscular, and strong. On them a torrid sun has burnt its deepest hue, their complexion being darker than that of any others in the island. Their features are regular, and occasionally prominent; their countenance open and prepossessing; their eyes dark, and their glance keen and piercing; their hair black and shining, often long, though the crisped or curly hair occurs more frequently among them than the inhabitants of other provinces. Their aspect is bold and imposing, their step firm though quick, and their address and movements often graceful, and always unembarrassed.

The God of nature has so liberally supplied their wants with his bounties of spontaneous growth, in their soil, that, unless roused by strong excitement, the habits of the Sakalavas, like those of other uncivilized countries, incline to indolence rather than activity. Summoned to war, especially to defensive war, they are prompt, energetic, resolute, and daring; but, the storm passed, the immediate danger removed, or surrounded with peace, and dwelling in security, they surrender themselves to a state of comparative indolence ; and become the too-willing victims of the delusions by which their race are more strongly spell-bound than most of the other natives of Madagascar — charms, divination, and sorcery.

Towards Europeans, the Sakalavas have generally cherished sentiments of friendship, entertaining an exalted opinion of their superiority. And though themselves degraded at present by their childish superstitions, by their faith in witchcraft and all its endless absurdities, they yet exhibit ample proofs of mental powers capable, under proper culture, of the highest attainments: if enriched with the means of intellectual and moral improvement, they will, in all probability, rise, as others, once as dark, deluded, and degraded as they are, have emerged from barbarism, and attained eminence and moral worth among the nations. There is something in the very appearance of the Sakalava in his favour. His manly air and gait, his full countenance and penetrating look, declare him destined to something higher and nobler than he has yet attained. In ordinary intercourse, the Sakalavas discover much shrewdness, with less of cunning or deceit than many of their neighbours.

The Betsileo, a term signifying invincible, form a third distinct race in Madagascar; and though in some respects they resemble their neighbours and conquerors, the Hovas, in others they are distinct. They are generally low in stature, slender in figure, erect, and nimble in their movements; their colour is occasionally light copper, though frequently dark; their lips are thick, the eyes hazel, and their hair black, long, and curling. In these respects they approximate to the Hovas; but, in their patriarchal mode of life, modest unassuming address, the absence of anything like a bold and martial bearing in aspect or behaviour, their attachment to the peaceful labours of agriculture, want of that energy, enterprise, and cunning which have made the Hovas sovereigns of a large portion of the island, as well as in many of their manners and customs, they appear to be a different people, and seem to possess few, if any, traits of character which could have originated, or have justified the assumption of the name by which they are now distinguished.

The Betanimena and Betsimisaraka, already stated to be evidently but one people, constitute the next distinct and numerous portion of the inhabitants of Madagascar, differing in many respects from the Betsileo, as much as the latter do from their western neighbours the Sakalavas.

In stature, the Betanimena and Betsimisaraka resemble the Hovas, and, though in complexion rather darker, are, next to them, the fairest race in the island: their hair is generally frizzly, though not always black; their movements are less active than those of the inhabitants of the centre and western parts of the island; and though their limbs are strong and muscular, they exhibit only occasionally the bold and martial courage of the Sakalavas, or the enterprise, consciousness of power, and industry of the Hovas; though peculiarly distinguished by cleanliness in their houses and apparel, they seem, with comparatively few exceptions, to be degraded in morals below most of their countrymen, and are often the subjects of apathy and indolence in equal extremes. They are, however, in some respects an interesting people.

The inhabitants of the Isle of St. Mary's call themselves the descendants of Abraham — a designation most probably brought by some of the numerous pirates who, since the discovery of the island, have settled on its borders, and, intermarrying with the aborigines, have ultimately mingled their peculiar characters with those of the native inhabitants. The lineaments of European features, occasionally observable in the countenances of the

Betsimisaraka and the Betanimena, may probably have been derived from this early intercourse of the natives with Europeans.

In the province of Matitanana, the Arabs, who for centuries past have been accustomed to trade with the Malagasy, have their principal settlements; and this province is the chief residence of the people designated Zafindramina, descendants of the mother of Mahomet, from Zafy, descendants, and Amina, for "Imana," the mother of the prophet.

It is supposed that at some remote period, a number of Arabs, followers of the Prophet, settled in Matitanana, and, by intermarrying with the natives, became amalgamated with the original population, but gave to the descendants the distinctive name which they still bear. The Betsimisaraka is composed of the Zafibirihama, the Zafindramina blended with the aborigines of Matitanana and the adjacent provinces. This may account for the lightness of their colour, and the number of distinguished chiefs that have risen up among them. Without specifying others, we may mention the late Jean Rene,

Fisatra, and Prince Corroller, who were of the race of the Zafindramina.

The Bezanozano, "anarchical," are the next tribe that requires notice. They are not numerous, yet seem to be totally distinct from the Betsimisaraka on the one hand, and the Hovas on the other. They are not tall, but remarkably stout; their neck is short, their bust full, their colour black, their features flat, their hair occasionally curly, but most frequently approaching to the frizzly or crisped appearance. Their joints are stiff, and their movements heavy: they are considered the best coolies, or bearers of burdens, in the country. They exhibit many commendable traits of character, manifest frequently great decision and firmness, with independency of action, and a fondness for domestic life. Polygamy prevails to a very limited extent, and their morals appear superior to those of many other tribes.

The Antsianaka, "not subjects of others," though regarded as a distinct race, appear to resemble the last tribe in its most distinguishing peculiarities. They are black in colour, short in stature, and firmly set; their limbs are strong.

The Antsianaka are more numerous than the Bezanozano ; and however independent they may at one time have been, they are now easily held in subjection by the Hovas.

The power of disciplined troops, and the comparative weakness of mere numbers, were strikingly evinced in a fact which lately occurred in this province; in which it is stated, that three thousand of the natives were successfully opposed and routed hy Jive soldiers. It is reported, that at the first shot one of the three thousand was killed, and that the rest, probably expecting a similar fate, instantly fled.

The above are the principal races or tribes recognized by the people themselves; and though there are others, especially in the southern parts of the island, with which we are less familiar than with those already described, they are inferior in number and importance, and are rather branches of them than distinct tribes.

Physically considered, the various nations inhabiting Madagascar appear to form two distinct races, in many respects totally dissimilar, and having each a separate and probably remote origin. Between these races the distinction of colour is marked and permanent. The peculiarities of the dark race are, a black complexion, and a taller stature than the olive-coloured tribes, stouter body, thick projecting lips, curly or frizzly hair, a frank and honest bearing, or a grave or timid expression of countenance ; some of the tribes exhibiting a full bust, resembling the Africans on the Mozambique shore.

The fairer race, including the Hovas, and many individuals among the Betsileo, the Betsimisaraka, and Betanimena, but especially the Hovas, are distinguished by a light olive or copper skin, smaller stature, long hair, dark hazel or black eyes, erect figure, courteous and prepossessing address, active movements, with an open and vivacious aspect.

All the tribes have naturally fine and regular teeth, beautifully white, which is to be ascribed to their practice of washing them regularly, and cleaning or bleaching them by the use of a dye, or pigment, made from the *laingio*, a native plant. The former race probably emigrated, at some remote period, from the adjacent coast of Africa. The latter have evidently one origin in common with that singular and astonishing race whose source is yet involved in mysterious uncertainty, but

"Whose path was on the mountain wave;
Whose home was on the sea;"

whose spirit of adventurous enterprise led them, at a period when navigation was almost unknown in Europe, to visit the borders of Africa and of Asia, and whose descendants now people the shores of the straits of Malacca, the Malayan archipelago, and the chief clusters of the Polynesian islands.

We have no better means of ascertaining the period at which the distinct tribes now inhabiting Madagascar arrived on its shores, than we have of tracing the several races to the sources of their origin. The dark-coloured natives appear to have been the earliest settlers in the island, and may therefore be considered as the aborigines of the country, as tradition respecting the settlement of the fairer race invariably represents them as having, at the time of their arrival, found the country inhabited. Their languages do not assist the inquiry, for they have been so intimately blended, as to present, in those spoken by the distinct races respectively, fewer peculiarities than are in other points observable among those by whom they are used.

We have already seen that the physical peculiarities of the several tribes now constituting the population of Madagascar, are considerably diversified; and serviceable as an acquaintance with their distinctions might be, in aiding our inquiries into the origin of the nations now peopling our globe, and the means and the course by which many tribes of the human family reached the countries which they now inhabit, these points are, when the mental and moral qualities of the people are regarded, comparatively unimportant. We contemplate their intellectual habits and powers, and their peculiarities of mind, with greater satisfaction, and derive from these, when viewed in connexion with their physical constitution, new evidence, not only of the fact that God has made of one blood all the nations that dwell on the face of the earth, but that He has endowed them with faculties of a corresponding order; and that while the same variety is observable in this as in other portions of the Creator's workmanship, all the essential elements of our intellectual nature belong equally to the several portions of mankind ; and that the elevation, strength, and vigour these attain in some, and the imbecility and prostration to which they have sunk in others, are to be ascribed to the culture bestowed and the direction given to the one, and the neglect, indolence, and vice by which the other is degraded and destroyed. And though the lineaments of their character shew, with affecting distinctness, how largely they have shared in the calamities which sin has inflicted on our race, a knowledge of this will not diminish our concern for their welfare, nor repress our desires to become more intimately acquainted with their circumstances.

Chapter IV

Although the natives of Madagascar have been frequently-represented as destitute of any national system of religion, as having no popular idols, or religious observances, towards which they evinced any strong predilection, and might therefore be regarded as a people favourably prepared for the reception of Christianity, being unawed by an interested priesthood, and unprejudiced in favour of any ancient creed, their actual circumstances will be found to differ widely from this flattering, but too hastily formed opinion.

The Malagasy, possessing the feelings and passions which are common to human nature, and being subject to the same hopes and fears, joys and sorrows, as other members of the human family in their destitution of the light and guidance of revelation, have endeavoured, like others similarly circumstanced, to find resources which might satisfy the cravings of the mind, and allay the feverishness of a bewildered imagination, which might arm them with fortitude amidst the apprehensions of mysterious and undefined evils, and inspire them with hope in the prospect of some unknown and equally undefined futurity. The operation of an invisible agency, or of different agencies, they see demonstrated in the phenomena, the order, and the formation of the universe around them. Yet strangers to the sublime idea of a superintending Providence, and almost equally strangers to any rational and philosophical explanation of daily occurring natural phenomena, they promptly attribute everything to the influence of charms (ody), which their imaginations invent, possessing qualities and virtues adequate to the production of all the varied effects either witnessed or experienced.

Still, while a belief in the efficacy of these potent charms seems to constitute one of the principal articles of their creed, it does not constitute the whole. It forms an important part of the Malagasy system of belief, but it is only a part. It is, in the minds of these credulous people, intimately associated with a conviction of the infallibility of the sikidy, or divination, by which the charm, according to its particular kind or design, in any given case, must be decided. And this again is as closely blended with a belief in some superior power, whose will or fiat is ascertained by the operation of the diviner's art — an art, by which, from premises avowedly laid in chances, a process is worked out by rule, and an indubitable certainty educed as the result.

Yet as firmly as the devout believers in the Koran adhere to the paralyzing doctrine of fate, do the Malagasy tenaciously maintain their "vintana" — a stern, unbending, fixed, immutable destiny; and after all they have pleaded for their charms, or sikidy, or god, everything is summed up with them in one comprehensive ultimatum — " Izany ny vintany" — " Such was his destiny or fate."

Madagascar, it is true, exhibits no outward and visible objects of worship, calculated to charm the senses or claim the veneration of the inhabitants of the country. It recognizes no order of priesthood, and has no classic associations with objects of long-established adoration. But it is not without its idols, its ceremonies, its sacrifices, and its divinations.

It has its altars too, its vows, and its forbidden things — forbidden, because hateful to the imaginary genius of the place. It has its mythology, crude as it is, and its guardians of the gods, all impoverished as they are. It has its supplications, deprecations, oaths, and forms of benedictiou.

It has also, as may justly be imagined, its full share of puerile credulity in ghosts, spirits, and apparitions, and in the legendary wonders and feats of giants and other monsters of former days. It makes its appeal by ordeal to some superior power, for preservation from the malevolent though unenviable craft of the sorcerer; and in order that the land may be purged from the evils of witchcraft, it is imbued with the innocent blood of the unfortunately suspected victim — poisoned, speared, strangled, or dashed over the fatal precipice. In a word, the Malagasy are heathen, destitute of the volume of divine truth, and in its absence carefully observing the faith, institutions, and traditions of their ancestors. Vague, absurd, and unsatisfactory as their creed may be, they cling to it with unyielding tenacity. Dark and perplexed as are their minds on the great principles of true religion, they are not without thoughts and feelings on the subject. Their minds are not a blank, upon which truth may at once be inscribed in legible characters, but filled with vain imaginations, erroneous fancies, crude conceptions, superstitious fears, and a pertinacious adherence to the opinions and decisions of their ancestors.

In investigating the religious faith and practice of the Malagasy, a primary question is — do they believe in, or have they any knowledge of, the one true God, the Maker and Preserver of all things? A cursory observation would, probably, induce a favourable answer; for they speak of God, they pray to God, they appeal to God, and they bless in the name of God. But if the inquiry be pursued — if it be ascertained what ideas they attach to the term God, their opinions, if indeed they merit that appellation, will be found so vague, contradictory, and absurd, that the inquirer will be disposed to conclude that the Malagasy have no knowledge of Him who created the heavens and the earth, and who clothes himself with honour and majesty.

The terms in the native language for God are — Andria-manitra and Zanahary, or Andria-nanahary. The first and last are in most common use in the interior of the island, and Zanahary on the coast. By Andria-manitra is probably meant Prince of heaven, though by the analogy of the language the word would then be Andrian-danitra.

Strictly the word seems to be compounded of Andriana, "prince," and manitra, "sweet-scented" or perfumed, which affords no consistent idea as applied to the Supreme Being.

Zanahary means he who causes to possess — the source of possession and Andria-nanahary has the same signification, being the same word radically, with andriana, or prince, affixed to it.

If a Malagasy be asked the signification of these term?, he replies that he cannot tell. Ask him if they all mean the same thing, if they are different terms used to convey the same idea, and he answers " Yes," or he will perhaps say that Andria-manitra is the male god, and Zanahary the female. Name to him his idols, and he avows that they are andria-manitra, or, if rather more speculative than the general mass of the people, he will perhaps say, they are sampy, i.e. "helpers," or auxiliaries, all the idols being called sampy, helpers, at the same time that the word may also signify an object by which a solemn oath is taken, in which sense the king may say aza misampy ahy, i.e. "do not swear by me." If, however, a Malagasy be asked with respect to these sampy, whom they do help, the reply is vague and unsatisfactory. They help, andriamanitra — they help the people in going to war, in obtaining blessings, in recovering from diseases, &c. Then again, the genius invoked by the Malagasy in their ordeal of tangena, under the name of manamango, they also denominate and declare to be andriamanitra. The king they also call andria-manitra, and sometimes with the addition of hita maso — "seen by the eye," i.e. the visible god. In short, whatever is great, whatever exceeds the capacity of their understandings, they designate by the one convenient and comprehensive appellation, andriamanitra. Whatever is new and useful and extraordinary, is called god. Silk is considered as god in the highest degree, the superlative adjective being added to the noun — andriamanitra-indrindra. Rice, money, thunder and lightning, and earthquakes, are all called god. Their ancestors and a deceased sovereign they designate in the same manner. Taratasy, or book, they call god, from its wonderful capacity of speaking by merely looking at it Velvet is called by the singular epithet — son of god.

Many of the people when asked what is God? will reply : a star, the sun, the sky, money, or anything to which they attach notions of glory or mystery. Others have an obscure notion of God being a spirit, or rather a multitude of spirits, attending upon individual persons, and thus their language very often is — everyone has his god; the blind have a blind god, that makes them unable to see; the rich have a rich god, that enriches them; and the prayer offered to an idol consists generally of detached and brief sentences, simply entreating the bestowment of riches, bullocks, rice, health, or other temporal possessions.

It becomes a subject of interesting but almost hopeless inquiry, to whom do the Malagasy pray, and vow, and offer sacrifice? To Andria-manitra, to the Vazimba, and to their ancestors. Who sends the rain? Ramahavaly, one of the principal idols. And who withholds it? We do not know; perhaps god — perhaps the deceased king. But amidst all this confusion, who do the Malagasy believe created them and all things, and who sustains and governs all things?

The reply is, Andria-manitra; and to any question beyond this, the honest reply not unfrequently is — We do not know, we don't think about these things.

Still more vague and indefinite are the ideas they entertain respecting the human soul and its future existence.

British agent went to him, and inquired his reasons for doing so. "Oh," said the king, "we are answering one another — both of us are gods. God above is speaking by his thunder and lightning, and I am replying by my powder and caimon." Mr. Hastie pointed out to him the presumption of his conduct; and the king ordered the firing to cease.

They have no knowledge of the doctrine of the soul as a separate, immaterial, immortal principle in man, nor has their language any word to express such an idea. They speak of the saina, but mean by this the intellectual powers. They speak also of the fanahy, the nearest term found to express spirit; but it seems, in their use of it, to imply principally the moral qualities or dispositions. In almost the same breath, a Malagasy will express his belief that when he dies he ceases altogether to exist, dying like the brute, and being conscious no more, and yet confess the fact, that he is in the habit of praying to his ancestors! If asked, were his ancestors not human beings like himself, and did they not cease altogether to exist when they died — how then can it be consistent to pray to them when they have no longer any being, he will answer. True, but there is their matoatoa, their ghost; and this is supposed to be hovering about the tomb when the body is interred. And there is also the ambiroa, or apparition, upposed to announce death, to visit a person when about dying, and to intimate to him, and sometimes to others, his approaching dissolution, an idea by no means peculiar to Madagascar, as it corresponds with the popular superstition of most European countries, that the funeral, or apparition, of a person still living, is permitted to be seen as a supernatural intimation of his approaching death.

The next question is. What becomes of the saina, or mind, when a person dies? To which the Malagasy replies. It is a part of the body. But does it return to dust with the body in the grave? No; the body returns to dust, and the saina becomes levona, i.e. "vanished," invisible.

And the aina, or life, becomes rivotra — air, or wind, not retaining its individuality, but absorbed and lost in mere aura — a mere breeze — a breath in the general mass of air floating around. And what becomes of the fanahy? It remains — it exists but only in the associations of memory — a mere idea or recollection, therefore a metaphysical entity.

Hence the word comes to signify character; and so far as a man's character and dispositions may be held in the remembrance of survivors, his "fanahy" is said to remain.

But this is obviously a very loose application of the term.

It has been said that the Malagasy believe in the existence of four superior divinities or lords, governing respectively the four quarters of the earth. An idea of this kind certainly prevails on some parts of the coast, but in the interior it is regarded as fabulous.

Such being the opinions of the Malagasy concerning God and the human soul, it is obvious that the doctrine of a future state of retribution is unknown amongst them.

No conceptions are entertained on the subject of the relations subsisting between the Creator and his creatures; and hence no impressions exist respecting moral responsibility and its specific moral obligations. The exercise of the domestic, social, and civil virtues depend upon the frail basis of the customs of antiquity, and the established usages of the country. These at least serve as their guide and standard while they are enforced by the sanction of the law, and the enactments of the sovereign.

Hence it may easily be inferred how egregiously erroneous will be the comparative scale of virtues and vices as drawn by a Malagasy. Chicanery, lying, cheating, and defrauding, are mere trifles compared with the enormous offences of trampling or dancing upon a grave, eating pork in certain districts where it is prohibited, running after an owl or a wild cat, or preparing enchantments.

The weekly computation of time, the ceremony of circumcision, various purifications, and the offering of sacrifices, are almost the only circumstances found among the Malagasy corresponding with those of the Mosaic institutes. No traditional knowledge appears to exist amongst them of any of the great events unfolded to the world by the inspired records, such as the creation, the fall of man, the deluge, the selection of one favoured people, the performance of miracles, or the promise of a Deliverer for the human race. It may be almost superfluous to add, that no ideas, however confused or remote, are found to exist relating to the doctrine of a Mediator, the advent of the Redeemer, the salvation of man, the renewal of the heart, the resurrection of the dead, the judgment to come, or the glory to be revealed.

Chapter V

The development of the Christian religion in Madagascar[4].

The religion of the Malagasies appears to be fundamentally a kind of mixed Monotheism, under the form of a Fetishism which finds expression in numerous superstitious practices of which these people are very tenacious. Even those who have received Christian instruction and baptism retain a tendency to be guided, in the various circumstances of their lives, rather by these superstitious prescriptions than by the dictates of reason and faith. They admit the existence of the soul, but without, apparently, forming any very exact notion of it; in their conception, it is not so much a spirit made in the image of the Creator as a double of the man, only more subtile than the visible corporeal man.

The Malagasy is naturally prone to lying, cupidity, and sexual immorality, which is for

---

[4] By Paul Camboué.

him so far from being a detestable vice that parents are the first to introduce their children to debauchery. This immorality and the lack of stability and fidelity in marriage are the great obstacles to the development of the family and of the Christian religion in Madagascar.

The first priests to bring the Gospel of Jesus Christ to Madagascar after the discovery of the island, came with the Portuguese. Old documents mention religious who, about the year 1540, accompanied a colony of emigrants to the south-eastern part of the island, where they were all massacred together during the celebration of a feast. Then again, about 1585, Frey Joao de S. Thome, a Dominican, appears to have been poisoned on the coast of the island.

In the seventh century two Jesuits came from Goa with Ramaka, the young son of the King of Anosy. This youth had been taken away, in 1615, by a Portuguese ship, to Goa, where the viceroy had entrusted him to the care of the Jesuits; he had been instructed and baptized. Ramaka's father permitted these two Jesuits to preach Christianity in his dominions. But soon, when they were beginning to wield some power for good, the king, instigated by his *ombiasy* (sorcerers) forbade his subjects to either give or sell anything whatsoever to the fathers. One of the two died, but the other succeeded in returning to India. Some years after this, the Lazarists, sent by St. Vincent de Paul, essayed to conquer Madagascar for the Faith. The *Societe de l'Orient* had then recently taken possession, in the name of France, of a tract of territory on the south-eastern littoral, and had named its principal establishment Fort-Dauphin. The first superior of this Lazarist mission was M. Nacquart; he left France with the Sieur de Flacourt, who represented the *Societe de l'Orient*, and one of his associates, M. Gondree. Arriving at Fort-Dauphin in December, 1648, M. Nacquart devoted himself most zealously, amid difficulties of every kind, to the evangelization of the natives, until he was carried off by a fever, 29 May, 1650. M. Gondree had died the year before. During these fourteen months of apostolate seventy-seven persons had received baptism. It was not until four years later that MM. Mounier and

Bourdaise came to continue the missionary work which had been initiated at such cost; but they too, succumbed to the severity of their task. A reinforcement of three missionaries sent to their assistance never reached them; one died at sea, the other two on the island of St. Mary, where they had landed. Nevertheless, St. Vincent de Paul was not discouraged.

In 1663 M. Almeras, the successor of St. Vincent de Paul in the government of the Congregation of St. Lazare, obtained the appointment of M. Etienne as prefect Apostolic and sent him to Fort-Dauphin with two of his brethren and some workmen. On Christmas Day M. Etienne baptized fifteen little children and four adults. But it was not long before he, too, fell a victim to his zeal. On 7 March, 1665, four new missionaries set out, and on 7 January, 1667, they were followed by five priests and four lay brothers, with two Recollet fathers. But in 1671, the Compagnie des Indes, which had succeeded to the Societe de l'Orient, having resolved to quit Madagascar, M. Jolly, M. Almeras' successor, recaled his missionaries. Only two out of thirty-seven who had been sent to theisland, were able to return to France, in June 1676; all the rest had died in harness. From the forced abandonment of the Madagascar mission in 1674 until the middle of the nineteenth century, there were only a few isolated attempts, at long intervals, to resume the evangelization of the great African Island: we may mention those of M. Noinville de Glefier, of the Missions Etrangeres of Paris, and of the Lazarists Monet and Durocher. The last-named even sent some natives to the Propaganda seminary in Rome with the view of training them for the apostolate in their own country.

In 1832 MM. de Solages and Dalmond laid the first foundations of the new Madagascar Mission. But by this time some English Methodists, supported by the Government of their country, had already succeeded in establishing themselves in the centre of the island. The Rev. Mr. Jones had obtained authorization from the Court of Imerina to open a school at Tananarivo, the capital. Other English Protestant missionaries followed him, and by 1830 they had thirty-two schools in

Imerina, with four thousand pupils. When, moreover, it was learned at Tananarivo that the new prefect Apostolic, M. de Solages, a Catholic priest, was on his way to the capital, everything was done to arrest his progress, and he died of misery and grief at Andovoranto. M. Dalmond took up the work begun by M. de Solages. After preaching the Gospel in the small island off the coast until about 1843, he returned to France in order to recruit a large missionary force. The aid which he so much needed he obtained from Father Roothan, the general of the Jesuits, who authorized him to take six fathers or brothers from the Lyons province. Two priests from the Holy Ghost Seminary went with them. After a fruitless attempt at Saint-Augustin, the Jesuit fathers set themselves to evangelize the adjacent islands of St. Mary, Nosi-Be, and Mayote. Assisted by the Sisters of St. Joseph of Cluny, they also made earnest efforts towards the instruciton and education of the Malagasy boys and girls in the island of Reunion (or Bourbon). They did not, however, by any means lose sight of the great island, and again endeavoured to establish themselves on its littoral, but were once more compelled to abandon their brave enterprise.

It was only in 1855 that Pere Finaz, disguised, and under an assumed name, was able to penetrate as far as the capital. "At last", he exclaimed in the joy of his heart, "I am at Tananarivo, of which I take possession in the name of Catholicism." Waiting for the time when he should be able to freely announce the Gospel to the Hova, he used all his efforts to prolong his stay at the capital without arousing suspicion, making himself useful and agreeable to the queen and the great personages of the realm. He sent up a balloon before the awe-stricken populace assembeld in the holy place of Mahamasina; he contrived theatrical performances on a stage constructed and set by himself; he made them a telegraphic apparatus, a miniature railroad, and other things wonderful in their eyes. Meanwhile, Fathers Jouen and Weber, under assumed names, joined Father Finaz at Tananarivo, coming as assistants to a surgeon, Dr. Milhet-Fontarabie, who had been summoned from Reunion by the Queen of Madagascar, Ranavalona I, to perform a rhinoplastic operation on one of her favourites. But this state of affairs was not to last long; Ranavalona soon grew suspicious and ordered the expulsion of the few Europeans who resided at Tananarivo. The fathers, however, had managed, during their brief stay at the capital, to conciliate the favour of the heir presumptive, Ranavalona's son. And so it was that, in 1861, when this same prince, on the death of his mother, succeeded to the thone as Radama II, Fathers Jouen and Weber could return to Tananarivo, bringing with them a small contingent of Jesuit fathers and Sisters of St. Joseph of Cluny, and without being obliged, this time, to dissembel their object in coming.

Radama II gave full authorization for the teaching of the Catholic religion in his dominions; and this much having been conceded to the French Catholic missionaries, similar concessions had to be made to the English Protestants of the London Missionary Society. What with the large subventions furnished by this organization to its emissaries, and the clever manoeuvres of some of them-particularly of Mr. Ellis-after the tragic death of

Radama II, the English missionaries acquired considerable influence with the new queen, Rasoherina, and her chief adviser, Rainilaiarivony, to the detriment of the Catholic missionaries. The latter, moreover, were few in number-six fathers and five lay brothers at Tananarivo, with two small schools for boys and one, under the Sisters of St. Joseph of Cluny, for girls; and at Tamatave, three fathers, one lay brother, and two sisters. Nevertheless, in spite of all difficulties, the number of neophytes increased and, especially after the arrival of the Christian Brothers in 1866, the schools took on fresh vigour. Already four parishes were in operation within the capital city, and the missionaries thought of extending their efforts outside. Father Finaz opened the missionary station at Antanetibe on 12 September, 1868; by the end of 1869, theity-eight gropus of neophytes had been formed, twenty-two chapels built, and twenty-five schools opened. Betsileo was occupied in 1871, then Ampositra and Vakinankaratra. A propaganda periodical, "Resaka", was founded. A leper-house was bilt to receive about one hundred patients. The sisters gave care and remedies to the large numbers who daily applied at their dispensary. A fine large cathedral of cut stone was erected in the centre of Tananarivo. When the war between France and the Hova broke out in 1883, the Catholic mission numbered 44 priests, 19 lay brothers, 8 Brothers of the Christian Schools, 20 Sisters of St. Joseph of Cluny (besides 3 native postulants and 3 novices), 346 native male, and 181 native female, teachers, 20,000 pupils, a laity amounting to 80,000, 152 churches and 120 chapels completed, and 11 churches and 43 chapels in course of construction. In the year ending July, 1882, there were 1161 baptisms of adults, 1882 infant baptisms, 55,406 confessions, 580 first communions, 45,466 ordinary communions, 860 confirmations, and 190 marriages. Sir Gore Jones, a British Admiral, whose testimony cannot be suspected of favourable bias, declared in 1883, in a report to his Government after a visit to the island made by its orders, that the Catholic missionaries, "working silently in Madagascar", were planting in that land "a tree far superior to all others".

On 17 May, 1883, Admiral Pierre took possession of Majunga in the name of France, and on 11 June of Tamatave. A formal order of the queen expelled all the Catholic missionaries and all French citizens. "Do not resist the queen's word", was the answer of the more responsible among the native Catholics when the fathers consulted them as to the course to be pursued. "To do so would be to compromise our future and, perhaps, to bring upon us more serious misfortunes. If you submit now, you will the more easily return later on." They left the centre of the island-at the same time leaving the native Catholics to their own resources-and went down to the coast. For two years, more or less, while hostilities lasted, the Malagasy Catholics, left without priests, were able to maintain their religion-thanks to the devotion and energy of Victoire Rasoamanarivo, a lady related to the prime minister, of the native Brother Raphael of the Congregation of the Christian Schools, and of some members of the Catholic Union. This organization, consisting of young Malagasies, shows a truly wonderful zeal in their efforts to make up for the absence of the fathers. Both in the city parishes and at the country stations, they made themselves ubiquitous, instructing and encouraging the neophytes. At Tananarivo they sang the choral parts of high Mass every Sunday, just as if the priest had been at the altar; and the native Government, compelled to admire their fidelity, permitted this exercise of devotion. On the first Sunday after the departure of the fathers, when the Catholics attempting to enter the cathedral were warned away, Rasoamanarivo said to the guards at the door: "If you must have blood, begin by shedding mine; but fear shall not keep us from assembling for prayer."

www.ingramcontent.com/pod-product-compliance
Lightning Source LLC
Chambersburg PA
CBHW031404040426
42444CB00005B/412